Level D • Book 2

D1383788

QuickReads®
A Research-Based Fluency Program

Elfrieda H. Hiebert, Ph.D.

MODERN CURRICULUM PRESS

Pearson Learning Group

Program Reviewers and Consultants

Dr. Barbara A. Baird
Director of Federal Programs/Richardson ISD
Richardson, TX

Dr. Kate Kinsella
Dept. of Secondary Education and Step to College Program
San Francisco State University
San Francisco, CA

Pat Sears
Early Child Coordinator/Virginia Beach Public Schools
Virginia Beach, VA

Dr. Judith B. Smith
Supervisor of ESOL and World and Classical Languages/Baltimore City Public Schools
Baltimore, MD

The following people have contributed to the development of this product:

Art and Design: Dorothea Fox, Tracey Gerber, Salita Mehta,
    Janice Noto-Helmers, Evelyn O'Shea, Dan Thomas

Editorial: Lynn W. Kloss

Manufacturing: Michele Uhl

Marketing: Connie Buck

Production: Laura Benford-Sullivan, Jeffrey Engel

Publishing Operations: Jennifer Van Der Heide

Acknowledgments appear on page 9, which constitutes an extension of this copyright page.

Copyright © 2003 by Pearson Education, Inc., publishing as Modern Curriculum Press,
an imprint of Pearson Learning Group, 299 Jefferson Road, Parsippany, NJ 07054.
All rights reserved. No part of this book may be reproduced or transmitted in any form or
by any means, electronic, or mechanical, including photocopying, recording, or by any
information storage and retrieval system, without permission in writing from the publisher.
For information regarding permission(s), write to Rights and Permissions Department.

QuickReads® is a registered trademark of Pearson Education, Inc.

ISBN 0-7652-2781-9

Printed in the United States of America

11 12   08 07

Modern Curriculum Press

Pearson Learning Group

1-800-321-3106
www.pearsonlearning.com

Contents

Contents

SOCIAL
STUDIES
Our North American Neighbors

Contents

SCIENCE **Taking Care of Our Earth**

Contents

Acknowledgments

All photographs © Pearson Learning unless otherwise noted

Cover: James A. Sugar/Corbis

Interior: 3: M. K. Denny/PhotoEdit. 4: Tim Wright/Corbis. 6: Corbis. 7: John Cancalosi/Stock Boston. 8: Ian O'Leary/Getty Images, Inc. 10: t. Pictor International/PictureQuest; b. Neil Rabinowitz/Corbis. 12: Byron Jorjorian/Bruce Coleman Incorporated. 14: David Young-Wolff/PhotoEdit. 16: Sean Thompson/Getty Images, Inc./PhotoDisc, Inc. 18: Paul Conklin/PhotoEdit. 24: M. K. Denny/PhotoEdit. 26: Stuart Rosner/Stock Boston. 28: Jeff Greenberg/PhotoEdit. 30: Tim Wright/Corbis. 32: Mark Gibson/Index Stock Imagery, Inc. 40: R. Sidney/The Image Works. 42: Richard T. Nowitz/Corbis. 44: Robert Frerck/Odyssey Productions. 46: W. Kenneth Hamblin. 52: Yann Arthus-Bertrand/Corbis. 56: Corbis. 58: James L. Amos/Corbis. 60: Bill Ross/Corbis. 66: C. K. Lorenz/Photo Researchers, Inc. 70: John Cancalosi/Stock Boston. 72: Jan Halaska/Photo Researchers, Inc. 74: Jeff Greenberg/Photo Researchers, Inc. 80: Ian O'Leary/Getty Images, Inc. 86: Neil Ricklin/PhotoEdit.

Geography and How We Live

Alaska's polar climate (top) is very different
from Hawaii's tropical climate (bottom).

Climate Zones

A pattern of weather over a long time is called a climate. Earth has six major climate zones. The United States is large[25] enough to include examples of all six climate zones. Patterns of temperature and rainfall vary from one climate zone to another. As a result, the[50] clothes that people wear are often quite different in different climate zones.

People living in a tropical climate, such as Hawaii, do not need winter[75] coats. Temperatures are warm to hot all year. An umbrella can be handy, though, because Hawaii's tropical climate has heavy rains. In contrast, people living[100] in a polar climate, such as northern Alaska, need very warm coats because winter temperatures last for much of the year.[121]

Geography and How We Live

This man is growing corn in Iowa's continental climate.

Continental Climate

Iowa grows much of the world's popcorn. Crops such as corn grow well in Iowa's long, hot summers. Because it is in the[25] continental climate zone, Iowa's temperatures differ a lot from summer to winter. Summer temperatures can be as high as 100 degrees in the continental climate[50] zone. Winter temperatures can drop to 20 degrees below zero. Snow usually covers the ground in winter. People who live in the continental climate zone[75] need two sets of clothes—one for winter and one for summer.

A large part of the United States is in the continental climate zone.[100] Most places that are in the middle of the country have a continental climate. Some places near the ocean also are in this zone.[124]

Geography and How We Live

These people are riding in a parade in coastal California's warm winter.

Mild Climate

Areas near the ocean often have mild climates. In the mild climate zone, temperatures are similar in summer and winter. It doesn't get[25] very hot or cold at any time of the year.

Most of coastal California is in the mild climate zone. You need a calendar to[50] know when it's winter in coastal California because there is usually no snow. People spend a lot of time outdoors, even when the calendar says[75] it's winter. Unlike people in continental or polar climates, people in mild climates do not need warm winter clothes. In coastal California, however, people do[100] need umbrellas. Although yearly rainfall is less than it is in tropical climates, almost all of the rainfall occurs during the winter months.[123]

Geography and How We Live

The plants in the desert climate zone need very little rain to live.

Desert Climate

The desert climate zone includes places that are very hot and have very little rainfall. Most of Arizona, with its large areas of [25] desert, is in the desert climate zone. Around noon, the temperature in the desert climate zone can reach more than 100 degrees. Each year, part [50] of Arizona has more than 90 days when the temperature reaches at least 100 degrees.

Although the desert and polar climate zones are very different, [75] people living in both climate zones tend to spend a lot of time indoors during certain seasons. People in a desert climate zone, such as [100] Arizona, stay inside during the hottest months. People in a polar climate zone, such as Alaska, stay inside during the coldest months. [122]

Geography and How We Live

The snow and the people having a picnic show
the differences in the mountain climate zone.

Mountain Climate

In Colorado, you might need both winter and summer clothes on the same day. This is because much of Colorado is in the[25] mountain climate zone. How high in the mountains you are, or your altitude, can vary widely in the mountain climate zone.

In the mountain climate[50] zone, temperature and rainfall vary throughout the year. Temperature and rainfall depend on your altitude. At the base of the mountains, the climate could be[75] similar to the continental climate zone. Temperatures near the top of the mountains could be similar to the polar zone. In summer, the ground at[100] the highest altitudes could be covered with snow, while people wear shorts and T-shirts in the warm valleys at the base of the mountains.[124]

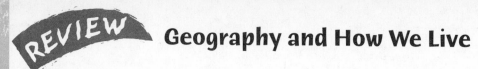

REVIEW Geography and How We Live

Write words that will help you remember what you learned.

Climate Zones

_____

_____

_____

_____

Continental Climate

_____

_____

_____

_____

Mild Climate

_____

_____

_____

_____

Desert Climate

_____

_____

_____

_____

Mountain Climate

_____

_____

_____

_____

Climate Zones

1. What is a climate?

   Ⓐ the kinds of clothes you wear

   Ⓑ bad weather

   Ⓒ a pattern of weather over a long time

   Ⓓ a thing to use to measure the weather

2. How are climate zones different from one another?

   _____

   _____

   _____

Continental Climate

1. Why do people who live in a continental climate need two sets of clothes?

   Ⓐ Days are very warm and nights are very cold.

   Ⓑ Sometimes it is rainy and sometimes it is dry.

   Ⓒ Winters are very cold and summers are very warm.

   Ⓓ They need one set of clothes for inside and one for outside.

2. Describe the continental climate zone.

   _____

   _____

   _____

Mild Climate

1. Another good name for "Mild Climate" is _____

   Ⓐ "Mild Weather All Year."

   Ⓑ "The State of California."

   Ⓒ "Rain in the Winter."

   Ⓓ "Hot Summer, Cold Winter."

2. Compare the winter and summer in the mild climate zone.

   _____

   _____

   _____

Desert Climate

1. "Desert Climate" is MAINLY about _____

   Ⓐ which animals live in the deserts of Arizona.

   Ⓑ why both Alaska and Arizona are in the desert climate zone.

   Ⓒ the kinds of clothes needed to live in Alaska and Arizona.

   Ⓓ the temperature and rainfall of the desert climate zone.

2. What is the desert climate zone?

   _____

   _____

   _____

Mountain Climate

1. The main idea of "Mountain Climate" is that _____

    Ⓐ temperatures and rainfall vary widely in the mountains.

    Ⓑ the climate in the mountains is cold throughout the year.

    Ⓒ the mountain climate is the same as the continental climate.

    Ⓓ the climate in the mountains is warm throughout the year.

2. Describe the mountain climate zone.

_____

_____

_____

Connect Your Ideas

1. What are two differences between two of the climates you read about?

_____

_____

_____

2. Why do you have to know about the climate of a place before you decide what to do or wear?

_____

_____

_____

Natural Resources and the Economy

Desks, books, and many other things used in this classroom are made from natural resources.

What Is a Natural Resource?

A natural resource is any material found on Earth that people use. People use many natural resources, including plants, animals,[25] rocks, and trees. Water and soil are natural resources, too. Water is used for drinking and washing. Water also provides a means for travel. Soil[50] is needed to grow plants and trees.

You don't have to look very far to see how natural resources are used. Your classroom has been[75] built from natural resources such as wood, rocks, and sand. The paper in books comes from trees. Pencils are made from wood and graphite. Graphite[100] is a mineral found in the ground. Even zippers, such as those on backpacks, are made from natural resources found in the ground.[123]

Natural Resources and the Economy

The wool from sheep is a renewable resource because it grows back after it is cut.

Renewable Resources

Some natural resources, such as trees, water, and animals, are renewable. Renewable resources are resources that can be used or made again. When[25] trees are cut down, new trees can be planted. When farmers take care of the soil, new crops can be grown. Rain refills rivers and[50] lakes. Cows continue to give milk, and sheep continue to provide wool when they are properly cared for.

However, natural resources can't be renewed if[75] they have been used up or ruined. For example, if all of one kind of tree is cut down, there will be no seeds to[100] make new trees. Growing too many crops in one place can ruin the soil, too. Resources are renewable only if people use them carefully.[124]

Natural Resources and the Economy

Most cars run on gas, which is a non-renewable natural resource.

Non-Renewable Resources

The temperature inside your school or home is controlled by a system that probably uses a natural resource such as coal, oil,[25] or natural gas. Coal, oil, and natural gas were formed inside Earth over millions of years. These resources were made from the remains of plants[50] and animals. Once coal, oil, natural gas, and minerals are used, they cannot be replaced. Natural resources that can't be replaced are called non-renewable[75] resources.

New inventions make it possible to get oil from beneath the ocean. Even with such new inventions, oil must not be wasted. This is[100] because once non-renewable natural resources are used up, they are gone forever. That is how non-renewable resources are different from renewable resources.[124]

Natural Resources and the Economy

The wool yarn in this picture will be used in a factory to make sweaters.

Using Natural Resources

Natural resources are used to make products such as sweaters, toys, and thousands of other things. Factories use natural resources to make[25] these products.

Most people buy sweaters that are made in factories instead of making sweaters themselves. However, someone does make these sweaters. Wool is spun[50] into yarn, and yarn is made into sweaters.

When people sell or buy products such as sweaters, for example, they can help a country's economy.[75] A country's economy is the way the country makes and gives out its products and services. Services are work that is done for others. Buying[100] and selling products and services adds money to a country's economy. Using natural resources wisely can also make a country's economy strong.[122]

Natural Resources and the Economy

Big ships like this one are used to import and export products.

Trading and the Economy

Countries trade natural resources and products with one another. This trading brings products and money into a country's economy. Exports are[25] the natural resources or products that go out of a country. Imports are the natural resources or products that come into a country.

The United[50] States uses natural resources to make products such as cars, computers, and food. It sells some of these products as exports. The United States also[75] buys products as imports that are made with the natural resources and products of other countries. For example, the United States imports clothing from China[100] and TV sets from Japan. The United States imports and exports thousands of products every year. Trading adds money and products to our economy.[124]

Natural Resources and the Economy

Write words that will help you remember what you learned.

What Is a Natural Resource?

_____

_____

_____

_____

Renewable Resources

_____

_____

_____

_____

Non-Renewable Resources

_____

_____

_____

_____

Using Natural Resources

_____

_____

_____

_____

Trading and the Economy

_____

_____

_____

_____

What Is a Natural Resource?

1. "What Is a Natural Resource?" is MAINLY about _____

   Ⓐ how to protect plants, animals, and trees.

   Ⓑ what natural resources are and how people use them.

   Ⓒ why people should use natural resources.

   Ⓓ all of the plants and animals found on Earth.

2. What is a natural resource?

   _____

   _____

   _____

Renewable Resources

1. What is a renewable resource?

   Ⓐ a resource that can be used or made again

   Ⓑ something that people use carefully

   Ⓒ soil and water that are used to grow crops

   Ⓓ trees that have been cut down

2. When can't a natural resource be renewed?

   _____

   _____

   _____

Natural Resources and the Economy

Non-Renewable Resources

1. A non-renewable resource is a resource that _____

   Ⓐ can be replaced after it is used.

   Ⓑ is made from plants and animals.

   Ⓒ cannot be replaced after it is used.

   Ⓓ is made from coal, oil, and natural gas.

2. What is the difference between renewable and non-renewable resources?

   _____

   _____

   _____

Using Natural Resources

1. Another good name for "Using Natural Resources" is _____

   Ⓐ "How to Make Sweaters in Factories."

   Ⓑ "Natural Resources and the Economy."

   Ⓒ "Factories and Renewable Resources."

   Ⓓ "Making Natural Resources in Factories."

2. How can using natural resources wisely help a country's economy?

   _____

   _____

   _____

Trading and the Economy

1. The main idea of "Trading and the Economy" is that _____

    Ⓐ many countries give their natural resources to other people.

    Ⓑ many countries import cars from the United States.

    Ⓒ trading natural resources and products helps a country's economy.

    Ⓓ the United States does more trading than any other country.

2. What are exports and imports?

_____

_____

_____

Connect Your Ideas

1. Tell about how you use three natural resources every day.

_____

_____

_____

2. What are two ways you can use natural resources wisely?

_____

_____

_____

Our North American Neighbors

This map shows the countries of Canada, the United States, and Mexico in North America.

Three North American Countries

You live in a country called the United States of America, which is in North America. Canada is the northern neighbor[25] of the United States, and Mexico is its southern neighbor.

With almost four million square miles, Canada is the second-largest country in the world.[50] Although Canada has a lot of land, its population is small. Canada has only about 30 million people. Mexico has about one-fifth the land[75] area of Canada. However, Mexico's population of 100 million is more than three times the population of Canada. The United States is smaller in land[100] area than Canada, but it is larger than Mexico. There are almost ten times as many people in the United States as there are in Canada.[126]

Many signs in Canada are written
in both English and French.

Comparing Canada and the United States

Canada and the United States are similar in many ways. Both countries stretch for thousands of miles from one [25] ocean to another. The Rocky Mountains and the Great Plains are in the middle of both countries.

Most people in both countries speak English because [50] each country had many settlers from England. Canada also had many settlers from France. In some parts of Canada, most people speak French. Many signs [75] in Canada are written in both English and French.

Like Americans, Canadians elect representatives to govern them. However, the two countries choose their leaders differently. [100] Americans elect a president. Canada's leader is called a prime minister. The leader of the group with the most elected representatives becomes Canada's prime minister. [125]

Our North American Neighbors

In Canada, many people enjoy winter
sports such as skating and sledding.

Canada's Winter Sports

In parts of Canada, the ground may be frozen and covered with snow for many months of the year. This cold weather[25] makes ice skating and hockey popular winter sports for Canadians. In small, northern towns, Canadian children skate and play hockey on outdoor ice rinks.

Hockey[50] has been popular in Canada since it was invented there more than 100 years ago. Today, hockey is popular in many other countries, including the[75] United States. Even places where it never snows, such as southern California, have professional hockey teams. The ice in these places is made in indoor[100] ice rinks. However, many professional hockey players on these teams learned to skate on outdoor ice rinks in small, northern Canadian towns.[122]

Our North American Neighbors

Many buildings in Mexico, such as this church,
were built by settlers from Spain.

Mexico and Its North American Neighbors

Compared to Canada and the United States, Mexico's land area is small. At some points, the East Coast and[25] the West Coast are close together. However, traveling can be difficult because Mexico has large mountain ranges on the East Coast and the West Coast.[50] Because of these mountain ranges, most of Mexico's population lives in the center of the country.

In addition, most people in the United States and[75] Canada speak English. However, most people in Mexico speak Spanish. This is because many of Mexico's settlers were Spanish. Also, Mexico's weather is warmer than[100] the weather in most of the United States and Canada. Parts of Mexico are so far south that it is warm all year.[123]

Our North American Neighbors

The Aztecs built cities and pyramids long before
the Spanish settlers arrived in Mexico.

Mexico City

Mexico's capital city, Mexico City, is famous for several reasons. First, Mexico City is the oldest city in North America. When the Spanish[25] arrived in North America more than 450 years ago, they found a city already there. People called the Aztecs had built the city, which had[50] some large pyramids. Today, visitors come from around the world to see the Aztec pyramids.

Mexico City is also famous for being the second largest[75] city in the world. More than 20 million people live in Mexico City. About one fifth of all Mexicans live in Mexico City.

Mexico City[100] is also the highest city in North America. At 7,350 feet high, Mexico City is almost one-and-a-half miles above sea level.[124]

Write words that will help you remember what you learned.

Three North American Countries

_____

_____

_____

_____

Comparing Canada and the United States

_____

_____

_____

_____

Canada's Winter Sports

_____

_____

_____

_____

Mexico and Its North American Neighbors

_____

_____

_____

_____

Mexico City

_____

_____

_____

_____

Three North American Countries

1. Another good name for "Three North American Countries" is _____

   Ⓐ "Large and Small Countries."

   Ⓑ "The Population of North America."

   Ⓒ "North American Neighbors."

   Ⓓ "The Many Countries of Canada."

2. Which country in North America is largest in land area? Which country is smallest?

   _____

   _____

   _____

Comparing Canada and the United States

1. "Comparing Canada and the United States" is MAINLY about _____

   Ⓐ how much larger the United States is than Canada.

   Ⓑ the governments of the United States and Canada.

   Ⓒ the kinds of people who settled the United States and Canada.

   Ⓓ ways the United States and Canada are similar and different.

2. Name two ways that Canada and the United States are similar. Name two ways that they are different.

   _____

   _____

   _____

Our North American Neighbors

Canada's Winter Sports

1. Which of these is a popular winter sport in Canada?

   Ⓐ hockey

   Ⓑ swimming

   Ⓒ baseball

   Ⓓ basketball

2. Retell what you learned in "Canada's Winter Sports."

   _____

   _____

   _____

Mexico and Its North American Neighbors

1. How is Mexico different from Canada and the United States?

   Ⓐ Mexico is smaller and its people speak Spanish.

   Ⓑ Mexico is always cold and Canada and the United States are always warm.

   Ⓒ Canada and the United States have many mountain ranges.

   Ⓓ It is easy to travel from the East Coast to the West Coast in Mexico.

2. Retell what you learned about Mexico in "Mexico and Its North American Neighbors."

   _____

   _____

   _____

Mexico City

1. The main idea of "Mexico City" is that _____

   (A) the people speak Spanish in Mexico City.

   (B) there are several reasons Mexico City is famous.

   (C) the Aztecs built some large pyramids in Mexico City.

   (D) most of the people in Mexico live in Mexico City.

2. What are three reasons Mexico City is famous?

   _____

   _____

   _____

Connect Your Ideas

1. Write two facts about each of the three countries of North America.

   _____

   _____

   _____

2. How is the weather different in Canada and Mexico?

   _____

   _____

   _____

Volcanoes

Extinct volcanoes like this one will never erupt again.

Kinds of Volcanoes

When you hear the word *volcano*, you probably think of red-hot lava pouring from a mountain. This idea is correct, at [25] least when the volcano is erupting. However, many volcanoes are extinct. An extinct, or dead, volcano will never erupt again.

Active volcanoes are another kind [50] of volcano. Active volcanoes are predicted to erupt again. The world has more than 1,500 active volcanoes. Some active volcanoes are quiet for hundreds of [75] years before they erupt again.

Some volcanoes have small eruptions. Others explode with great force, pouring out red-hot lava, ash, and gases. Today, volcanologists, [100] scientists who study volcanoes, can usually predict when a volcano will erupt. Sometimes, though, even volcanologists are surprised by a volcano. [121]

Volcanoes

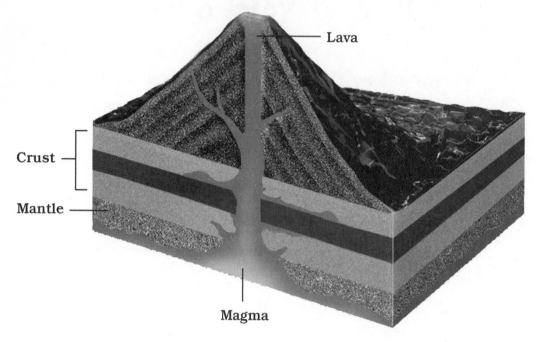

Lava

Crust

Mantle

Magma

Magma comes from deep within Earth's mantle.

How Volcanoes Form

A volcano is an opening in the crust, or outside layers, of Earth. The opening leads to a deeper layer of Earth [25] called the mantle. Think of Earth as a peach. The skin would be Earth's crust and the juicy part would be Earth's mantle. Earth's mantle [50] is made of white-hot rock called magma.

Earth's crust is broken into pieces called plates. When plates separate, a crack opens and magma escapes [75] as lava. Layers of lava form the volcano's cone. Then the volcano erupts, sending lava onto the land.

Volcanoes also form when plates move together [100] and overlap. The bottom plate sinks into Earth's mantle. Rock from the sinking plate melts into magma that is forced to the surface. [123]

Volcanoes

Erupting volcanoes can hurt trees and people many miles away.

When Volcanoes Erupt

A volcanic eruption happens when magma is forced up through a volcano. The magma that erupts from volcanoes is called lava. Lava[25] can reach a temperature of 2,000 degrees Fahrenheit. A temperature of 2,000 degrees Fahrenheit is almost four times hotter than the hottest setting on an[50] oven. As lava flows, it burns the plants and trees in its path. Even trees that are miles away can die because the heat from[75] the eruption dries out their sap.

Clouds of hot, poisonous gases from inside Earth also escape when a volcano erupts. These poisonous gases are dangerous[100] to breathe. An eruption's blast shatters cooled lava into tiny bits of ash. Volcanic ash can fall like snow for miles around.[122]

Volcanoes

This island in Hawaii is being formed
by a volcano on the ocean floor.

Volcanic Islands

The islands of Hawaii were formed by volcanoes that erupted from a hot spot in Earth's mantle. Hot spots are places where huge[25] amounts of magma build up in Earth's mantle and often erupt. Where Hawaii is now, ancient eruptions of lava flowed onto the ocean floor and[50] cooled to become hard rock. Later eruptions spilled new lava, and the rock grew.

With each eruption, the pile of cooled lava grew. When the[75] cooled lava reached the ocean's surface, an island was formed. As the plate moved above the hot spot, a new volcano formed and another island[100] began. By repeating this process, the hot spot slowly built a chain of islands. The state of Hawaii is made up of islands like these.[125]

Volcanoes

This lake was formed in an extinct volcano.

The Benefits of Volcanoes

Even though they cause harm, volcanoes have helped form our world. Billions of years ago, volcanoes were an important part of[25] how Earth's surface formed. Layers of rock from eruptions have made some volcanoes into tall mountains. Sometimes lakes formed in the spaces that were left[50] when rocks caved in or were blown away during volcanic eruptions.

People have found other benefits from volcanoes, too. One benefit is the beautiful gems[75] that sometimes form from minerals trapped in gas pockets of cooled lava. Also, volcanic ash is full of minerals that make soil better for growing[100] crops. Mount Vesuvius, a volcano in Italy, is famous for its grapes. The grapes of Mount Vesuvius grow on land that contains volcanic ash.[124]

Write words that will help you remember what you learned.

Kinds of Volcanoes

_____

_____

_____

_____

How Volcanoes Form

_____

_____

_____

_____

When Volcanoes Erupt

_____

_____

_____

_____

Volcanic Islands

_____

_____

_____

_____

The Benefits of Volcanoes

_____

_____

_____

_____

Kinds of Volcanoes

1. Another good name for "Kinds of Volcanoes" is _____

   Ⓐ "Red and Black Volcanoes."

   Ⓑ "Extinct and Active Volcanoes."

   Ⓒ "Lava and Ash Volcanoes."

   Ⓓ "Volcanologists Predict Eruptions."

2. Describe the two kinds of volcanoes.

   _____

   _____

   _____

How Volcanoes Form

1. How do volcanoes form?

   Ⓐ Two of Earth's plates make new mantle.

   Ⓑ Earth's crust is broken into plates.

   Ⓒ Earth's mantle flows into volcano magma.

   Ⓓ Lava flows out through Earth's crust.

2. What are two ways volcanoes form?

   _____

   _____

   _____

When Volcanoes Erupt

1. Why are volcanoes dangerous?

   Ⓐ People can lose lava when volcanoes erupt.

   Ⓑ Ash and hot gases cause cracks to form in Earth.

   Ⓒ Hot lava and poisonous gases can hurt living things on Earth.

   Ⓓ Hot lava can heat up the magma from Earth.

2. What happens when volcanoes erupt?

   _____

   _____

   _____

Volcanic Islands

1. "Volcanic Islands" is MAINLY about _____

   Ⓐ how every island is formed by volcanoes.

   Ⓑ how lava erupts inside the volcanoes in Hawaii.

   Ⓒ how the islands of Hawaii were formed.

   Ⓓ how volcanoes made hot spots in the islands of Hawaii.

2. How do volcanoes form an island?

   _____

   _____

   _____

The Benefits of Volcanoes

1. The main idea of "The Benefits of Volcanoes" is that _____

   Ⓐ volcanoes can cause bright light and beautiful lakes.

   Ⓑ fewer volcanoes are erupting today.

   Ⓒ volcanoes can do good things for Earth and its people.

   Ⓓ people today know how to stop volcanoes from erupting.

2. What are three benefits of volcanoes?

   _____

   _____

   _____

Connect Your Ideas

1. Retell three facts you learned about volcanoes.

   _____

   _____

   _____

2. How might Earth be different if there were no volcanoes?

   _____

   _____

   _____

Gila monsters need to live in hot deserts.

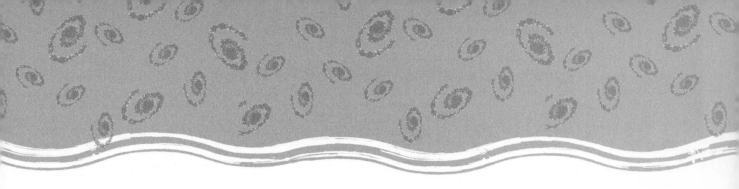

Ecosystems

Gila monsters live in hot deserts. This cold-blooded animal needs desert heat to survive. Gila monsters wouldn't survive in cold winters. Moose live[25] in northern forests where there are many evergreen trees and lakes. Without cool weather, lots of water, and woody plants, moose wouldn't survive.

Like all[50] plants and animals, moose and gila monsters have adapted to a certain setting, called a habitat or home. The larger area that includes habitats for[75] many animals and plants is called an ecosystem. Deserts and northern forests are examples of different ecosystems. An ecosystem includes all the plants, animals, and[100] non-living natural things, such as the rocks and soil, in an area. An ecosystem provides everything that the animals and plants need to live.[125]

Sunlight, plants, and animals work together to form a food chain.

Food Chains

The plants and animals in an ecosystem form a food chain. A food chain begins with plants because plants use sunlight to make[25] food. Animals can't make their own food, so they eat other things. Insects and rabbits eat plants. Then big birds eat the insects and rabbits.[50] So, the sunlight, plants, and animals form a food chain.

A food chain can break down when new animals invade an ecosystem. Here's what happened[75] in Australia. Beetles were eating sugarcane crops. Then sugarcane farmers brought giant toads from another country to eat the beetles. Because the toads were poisonous,[100] larger local animals wouldn't eat them. The poisonous toads broke the local food chain. Soon, there were too many giant toads in Australia.[123]

The giant armadillo is endangered
because its habitat is disappearing.

Endangered Species

Plants are an important part of an ecosystem. When too many plants are destroyed, animals lose their habitat. If the habitat for a [25] kind of animal, or species, gets too small, the entire species may become endangered because the animals can't find the things they need to live. [50] In this way, an endangered species can disappear from Earth.

Many species of animals live in the Amazon rain forest. In the last 30 years, [75] many rain forest trees have been cut down for lumber or to make roads or farms. The world's largest armadillo, the giant armadillo, is an [100] endangered species because its rain forest habitat is almost gone. Loss of the Amazon rain forest causes many animal species to become endangered. [123]

Taking Care of Our Earth

People around the world are working together
to save rain forests like this one.

Saving the Rain Forest

When a class of first and second graders in Sweden learned about the effects of destroying rain forests around the world,[25] they decided to work to save them. The children and their teacher learned that people could buy land in a rain forest for $25 an[50] acre. So they raised money by putting on shows and fairs. They also made and sold books and tapes about the rain forest.

By the[75] time these children were sixth and seventh graders, they had bought more than 2,000 acres of rain forest. Children from other countries who heard about[100] these Swedish children joined in. More than 33,000 acres of rain forest will not be destroyed because of what these Swedish children began.[123]

Taking Care of Our Earth

Recycling cans and bottles saves energy.

Recycle, Reuse, and Reduce

Garbage ends up in landfills that can leak chemicals into the water, soil, and air. These chemicals can harm plants, animals,[25] and people. When people reuse, recycle, and reduce materials, there is less garbage and Earth's ecosystems are not harmed.

Every American uses about 350 aluminum[50] cans each year. This aluminum can be reused by recycling it to make a new can. Recycling one aluminum can saves enough energy to run[75] a TV for three hours.

Another way to reduce demands on Earth's ecosystems is to turn off lights and TVs when they are not being[100] used. Turning off toys and flashlights that run on batteries helps, too. Chemicals from batteries are especially harmful to Earth's ecosystems.[121]

Taking Care of Our Earth

Write words that will help you remember what you learned.

Ecosystems

_____

_____

_____

_____

Food Chains

_____

_____

_____

_____

Endangered Species

_____

_____

_____

_____

Saving the Rain Forest

_____

_____

_____

_____

Recycle, Reuse, and Reduce

_____

_____

_____

_____

Ecosystems

1. Habitats are _____

   (A) the places where animals and plants live.

   (B) the non-living things in an area.

   (C) the living things in an area.

   (D) what plants and animals eat.

2. Why do gila monsters and moose live in different ecosystems?

   _____

   _____

   _____

Food Chains

1. "Food Chains" is MAINLY about _____

   (A) how new animals invade an ecosystem.

   (B) poisonous toads in Australia.

   (C) how plants and animals form a food chain.

   (D) how plants and animals use sunlight to make food.

2. Describe a food chain.

   _____

   _____

   _____

Endangered Species

1. Why is the giant armadillo endangered?

   Ⓐ Its home in the rain forest is almost gone.

   Ⓑ Too many people hunt the giant armadillo.

   Ⓒ Birds and plants have taken its habitat.

   Ⓓ People catch giant armadillos for zoos.

2. What is one way a species can become endangered?

   _____

   _____

   _____

Saving the Rain Forest

1. Another good name for "Saving the Rain Forest" is _____

   Ⓐ "Swedish Children Living in the Rain Forest."

   Ⓑ "Buying the Rain Forest to Save It."

   Ⓒ "Sixth and Seventh Graders in the Rain Forest."

   Ⓓ "The Swedish Rain Forest."

2. How did the Swedish school class help save the rain forest?

   _____

   _____

   _____

Recycle, Reuse, and Reduce

1. The main idea of "Recycle, Reuse, and Reduce" is that _____

   Ⓐ making less garbage helps the Earth's ecosystems.

   Ⓑ Earth's ecosystems can recycle aluminum cans.

   Ⓒ people put their garbage into landfills.

   Ⓓ Earth's ecosystems are not harmed by garbage.

2. How can recycling, reusing, and reducing help the environment?

_____

_____

_____

Connect Your Ideas

1. What animals and plants live in the habitat of your neighborhood?

_____

_____

_____

2. What are two things you could do to help take care of our Earth?

_____

_____

_____

Day and Night

Part of Earth is shown in daylight and
the other part is shown in darkness.

What Makes Day and Night?

Because light travels in a straight line in space, light from the Sun only falls on about half of Earth[25] at once. The part of Earth turned toward the Sun is lighted and the part turned away from the Sun is in shadow. If Earth[50] were not turning on its axis, one half of Earth would always be in daylight and the other half in darkness.

However, Earth does turn[75] on its axis once every 24 hours. As a result, the part of Earth that is in daylight changes. As Earth turns, each point on[100] its surface is lighted by the Sun, causing day. When Earth turns and that point passes into shadow, it's night.[120]

Day and Night

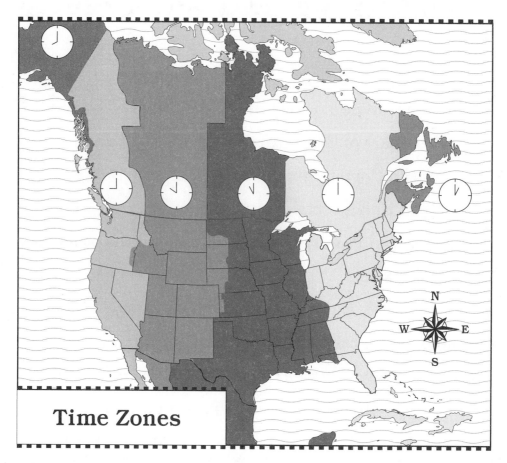

Time Zones

The clocks show the time zones in the United States and Canada.

Time Zones

Wherever you are on Earth, you know that the Sun rises in the morning and that noon is about the middle of the[25] day. However, when it's noon in New York, it's dark in Japan. Therefore, clocks in New York and Japan must show different times. To get[50] around this problem, people divided Earth into 24 time zones. A time zone is like a north-to-south slice of Earth. If you traveled[75] all the way around Earth at the middle, you would pass through all 24 time zones.

Large countries, such as the United States and Canada,[100] have several time zones. When it's 9:00 A.M. in California, it's 11:00 A.M. in Iowa and noon in New York.[120]

Day and Night

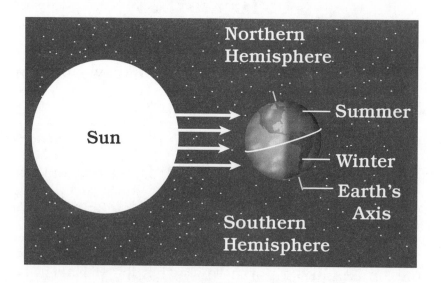

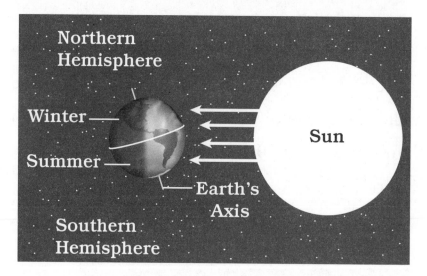

The top drawing shows summer in the Northern Hemisphere. The bottom drawing shows summer in the Southern Hemisphere.

Winter and Summer

Earth moves in a big oval around the Sun. Earth makes one orbit, or complete turn around the Sun, every year. While[25] Earth orbits the Sun, it also turns on its axis. Earth's axis and the Sun's axis are not at the same angle. As a result,[50] one half of Earth, or one hemisphere, tilts toward the Sun for part of the year and the other hemisphere tilts away from the Sun.[75]

The hemisphere that tilts toward the Sun stays in the Sun's light longer. This creates summer's longer, warmer days. Later in the year, Earth moves[100] to a new spot in its orbit. Then this hemisphere tilts away from the Sun. This creates winter's shorter, cooler days.[121]

Day and Night

Long shadows show that the Sun is low in the sky.

Shadows and Time

When sunlight falls on an object, the object's shadow points away from the Sun. The length and position of the shadow change[25] as the Sun appears to move across the sky. When the Sun is low in the sky, shadows are long. At noon, when the Sun[50] is high overhead, shadows are short.

People in ancient times did not have clocks. Then they noticed how shadows changed during the day, and they[75] built sundials that used shadows to tell time. A sundial is a disk with numbers around the edge that represent hours. An angled piece sticks[100] up from the center of the sundial and casts a shadow. You tell time by noting where the shadow falls on the sundial.[123]

Day and Night

The top drawing shows 1 A.M.
The bottom drawing shows 1 P.M.

A.M. and P.M.

Although a day has 24 hours, most clocks show only 12 hours. Clocks go around twice in one day. This means that [25] it is one o'clock at two times in every day, two o'clock at two times, and so on.

To tell these two times apart, the [50] letters "A.M." were added to the time to indicate the period from midnight to noon. The letters "P.M." indicate the period from noon to midnight. [75] "A.M." and "P.M." are abbreviations for the Latin phrases meaning "before noon" and "after noon." This means, for example, that the abbreviation 2 A.M. indicates [100] that it is 2 o'clock in the morning. The abbreviation 2 P.M. indicates that it is 2 o'clock in the afternoon. [121]

Day and Night

Write words that will help you remember what you learned.

What Makes Day and Night?

_____

_____

_____

_____

Time Zones

_____

_____

_____

Winter and Summer

_____

_____

_____

_____

Shadows and Time

_____

_____

_____

_____

A.M and P.M.

_____

_____

_____

_____

What Makes Day and Night?

1. What would happen if Earth did not turn on its axis?

   Ⓐ All of Earth would be in darkness all the time.

   Ⓑ All of Earth would be in daylight all the time.

   Ⓒ Half of Earth would always be in daylight and the other in darkness.

   Ⓓ Half of Earth would have long days and the other half would have short days.

2. What makes day and night?

   _____

   _____

   _____

Time Zones

1. "Time Zones" MAINLY tells about _____

   Ⓐ why people divided Earth into time zones.

   Ⓑ the number of time zones in the United States.

   Ⓒ how clocks work in Japan.

   Ⓓ why the sky is dark at night.

2. How do time zones help people tell time?

   _____

   _____

   _____

Day and Night

Winter and Summer

1. What causes summer?

   Ⓐ Part of Earth tilts toward the Sun.

   Ⓑ Earth's axis tilts away from the Sun.

   Ⓒ Part of Earth is heavier.

   Ⓓ The Sun shines on Earth for a shorter time.

2. Why are winter days colder than summer days?

   _____

   _____

   _____

Shadows and Time

1. The main idea of "Shadows and Time" is that _____

   Ⓐ the moon causes shadows.

   Ⓑ shadows change during the day.

   Ⓒ people today do not use sundials.

   Ⓓ shadows do not change with time.

2. Retell two facts you learned in "Shadows and Time."

   _____

   _____

   _____

A.M and P.M.

1. Another good name for "A.M. and P.M." is _____

    Ⓐ "Dividing the Day in Two."

    Ⓑ "Telling Time in Latin."

    Ⓒ "Twelve Hours in a Day."

    Ⓓ "How to Read a Clock."

2. Why do we have the abbreviations "A.M." and "P.M."?

_____

_____

_____

Connect Your Ideas

1. What are two ways that Earth's movements affect your life?

_____

_____

_____

2. Describe two different ways you can tell time.

_____

_____

_____

Reading Log · Level D · Book 2

	I Read This	New Words I Learned	New Facts I Learned	What Else I Want to Learn About This Subject
Geography and How We Live				
Climate Zones				
Continental Climate				
Mild Climate				
Desert Climate				
Mountain Climate				
Natural Resources and the Economy				
What Is a Natural Resource?				
Renewable Resources				
Non-Renewable Resources				
Using Natural Resources				
Trading and the Economy				
Our North American Neighbors				
Three North American Countries				
Comparing Canada and the United States				
Canada's Winter Sports				
Mexico and Its North American Neighbors				
Mexico City				

	I Read This	New Words I Learned	New Facts I Learned	What Else I Want to Learn About This Subject
Volcanoes				
Kinds of Volcanoes				
How Volcanoes Form				
When Volcanoes Erupt				
Volcanic Islands				
The Benefits of Volcanoes				
Taking Care of Our Earth				
Ecosystems				
Food Chains				
Endangered Species				
Saving the Rain Forest				
Recycle, Reuse, and Reduce				
Day and Night				
What Makes Day and Night?				
Time Zones				
Winter and Summer				
Shadows and Time				
A.M and P.M.				

Self-Check Graph

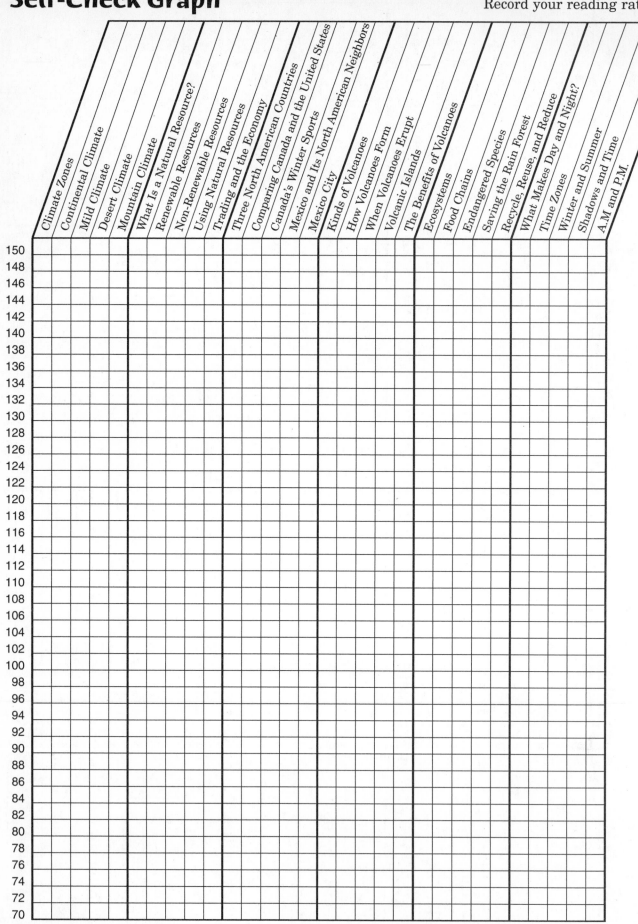